ESTHER HAUTZIG

Make It Special

Cards, Decorations, and Party Favors
for Holidays and Other Special Occasions

ILLUSTRATED BY MARTHA WESTON

Macmillan Publishing Company
NEW YORK

Collier Macmillan Publishers
LONDON

Macmillan Publishing Company
866 Third Avenue, New York, N.Y. 10022
Collier Macmillan Canada, Inc.
First Edition
Printed in the United States of America

10   9   8   7   6   5   4   3   2

The text of this book is set in 12 point Palatino.
The illustrations are rendered in pen-and-ink.

Library of Congress Cataloging-in-Publication Data
Hautzig, Esther Rudomin.
Make it special.
Summary: Provides suggestions and instructions for
making cards, decorations, party favors, and small
gifts for holidays, birthdays, and other special family
celebrations.
1. Holiday decorations—Juvenile literature.
2. Gifts—Juvenile literature.   [1. Holiday decorations.
2. Handicraft.   3. Gifts]   I. Weston, Martha, ill.
II. Title.
TT900.H6H38   1986   745.594'1   86-8616
ISBN 0-02-743370-6

FOR PHYLLIS LARKIN
a special person

Contents

Introduction

National or religious holidays, birthdays, and anniversaries are always special days. But other events can be just as meaningful to you and your family and close friends. When someone graduates from elementary school, comes in first in a spelling bee, wins a blue ribbon at the county fair, finishes a big project, or returns from a long business trip—that is also an important occasion and calls for a celebration.

With this book you can help make all the special days your family and friends mark look and feel festive. Helping to prepare for a party or a dinner—whether the guests are friends or "just family"—is a little like being part of an amateur theatrical production. For a show, announcements, props, and scenery are carefully chosen, and the audience, which may change each time, makes each performance different. The same is true for a party.

Designing your own greeting cards, helping to decorate the house, setting a cheerful and colorful table, making small party favors for family or guests—all of these can help to "stage" your show. They will also be a source of enormous pleasure for you, because there is nothing more gratifying and more loving than to create things with your own hands for happy events.

So please look in these pages for ideas on how special days can be made even more special, by a special person—*you!*

Before You Start

*W*hen a holiday or family celebration is coming up, look through this book ahead of time, decide which projects you may want to make, and review the lists of materials needed. If you keep a collection of odds and ends of decorative paper and fabric, ribbons, bits of jewelry, yarn, magazines, cardboard, and other valuable "junk," see if you can find what you may need there. If not, you'll have to start rounding up material from family, neighbors, friends, or your local shops.

Before you start working on a project, read all the instructions. Be sure you have allowed enough time to complete it. Set out all the materials and tools you will need on your working surface. There's no sense running around looking for something in the middle of your project! It's best to follow the instructions as closely as you can, but colors and sizes usually can be adjusted to suit yourself.

Use the illustrations as a guide, not as a strict rule. Designs and shapes can be varied to suit your own taste and skills.

Most of the gluing called for in the projects can be done with an all-purpose white glue, like Elmer's® Glue-All™, which is available anywhere and works beautifully on paper, wood, cloth, and other porous materials. A cement glue such as Duco or Sobo is best for metals, solid objects, and heavy trimmings, and I have indicated whenever that should be used. Macaroni, seashells, rice, beads, and feathers stick well to Elmer's® Dip 'n

Dab™ Glue; dried flowers, sequins, and glitter work best with Elmer's® Craft Bond™. Use glue sparingly. Work in a well-ventilated area and spread newspapers on your working surface.

When painting is called for, use water-based paints; they are safer and easier to clean up afterward. Read all the instructions on the cans of whatever paint you use; they are helpful and important. Work in a well-ventilated area and spread lots and lots of old newspapers on your working surface. Dip the brush in the paint halfway up the bristles, remove the excess, then apply the paint with short, even strokes. Immediately after you finish, clean your brush and put it away.

When using a knife or a single-edged razor blade, work on a thick layer of newspapers. If you have to cut a large piece of paper or fabric, put it down, hold it with one hand on top, and cut away from yourself. Regular scissors are fine for most projects. Small curved nail scissors are good to cut out designs in paper or fabric for greeting cards and small gifts.

Clean up scraps of fabric, paper, pasta, etc., after you finish. Save bits and pieces of material that can be used later.

Wear old clothes when you paint, glue, and do other fairly messy things. When you set the table, wash your hands beforehand, tie your hair if it's loose, and be neat while you work.

Dress nicely when your family expects guests. Shake hands with your parents' friends, and try to do whatever else you can to help your parents make company feel comfortable. It's a compliment to guests when you greet them with good manners, and you'll feel good about everything yourself, as well.

Have fun making it special!

Special Cards for Special Days

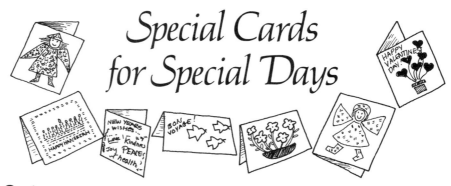

$\mathcal{M}$aking and sending cards is one of the most pleasant ways to anticipate a celebration. Cards from stores may be wonderfully funny or beautiful. But those you make yourself are truly special.

Many of the cards below can be used, with slight adjustments, for more than one holiday or occasion. For instance, those with flowers or hearts can be sent for birthdays and graduations as well as for Valentine's Day or Thanksgiving. Most of them can be used also as party invitations.

You can make cards from regular typing paper (which is now available in different colors) or use colored cards-by-the-pound (available in most stationery stores), unlined index cards, construction paper, or oak tag, which you can cut to any size. Colorful magazine pages, bits of ribbons and yarn, fabric scraps, and old photographs will be used for some of the designs.

Experiment before you make your final cards. They may be more attractive if you gain some experience through producing "samples"—and some of the early tries may turn out better than you expect. (Also, the materials are either free or very inexpensive!)

Be sure your cards will fit standard-size envelopes. Small Number 6 and long Number 10 envelopes are available in all stationery and dime stores. Square envelopes, called "baronial" envelopes, are sometimes harder to find, but most large stationers carry them in different sizes.

Cut the card stock to fit your envelopes or fold 8½-by-11-inch typing paper in various ways as shown on diagrams in this section. If you make self-mailing postcards from card stock that you cut yourself, make sure your cards conform to postal size regulations. These regulations can change, so check with the post office before you begin a project. Also, a card, mailed by itself or in an envelope, that weighs more than one ounce requires extra postage. When in doubt, take your cards to the post office and have them weighed before you stamp and mail them.

If you or your family receive pretty greeting cards made of sturdy paper, these can be recycled either as colorful postcards or notes. Just cut away the side of the card that was signed. The back of the picture on the greeting card can be used for writing a message of your own and sent as a postcard, provided the size conforms with postal regulations, or can be put in an envelope for mailing.

Design Cards

You can make a great variety of cards with scraps of various materials. The designs here are merely suggestions to start you thinking; it is your own ideas that will make your cards special. The instructions for making an angel can be adapted for making a scary witch on a Halloween card or party invitation. The instructions for making a flower or bird can be adapted for making a butterfly on a card or invitations for all kinds of celebrations.

MATERIALS: Construction or typing paper, unlined index cards, cards-by-the-pound, or other card stock; colorful pages from magazines, scraps of wallpaper, self-adhesive paper, gift-wrapping paper, or fabric; ribbons, yarn, sequins; cup or glass; pen or pencil, felt tip pens; scissors; glue.

INSTRUCTIONS:

Angels: Cut out shapes from decorative paper or fabric as shown in the illustration for an angel's body, wings, legs, and halo. Glue the shapes to the card. Use felt tip pens to draw the angel's face right above the body. As you draw blue, brown, or black eyes, a red mouth, and hair, you will find that each angel assumes its own personality—it really does!

You can vary the shapes of the angel's clothing, have the angel winged or wingless, halo-ed or halo-less, with hands folded together on the tummy or raised in a prayerful pose.

Flowers: To make a flower card, cut colorful paper into shapes like those suggested in the illustration. Glue the flower heads on the card in whichever way you like—as a single blossom, a loose bouquet of many little blooms, or a small group of three or four large flowers. Cut pieces of yarn or paper for stems and leaves and glue them in place. A pretty bow, either drawn with felt tip pens or cut from colorful paper and glued on, makes a nice finishing touch.

Birds: From decorative paper or fabric, cut out bird shapes like those in the illustration. Use solid colored paper for simple birds such as sparrows, colorful paper for birds that have bright plumage, and yellow felt for little chicks or ducks. Glue the birds' bodies to the card in any arrangement you like—a row of little sandpipers, or a group of sparrows, or a pair of ducks. Draw the heads, feet, eyes, and beaks with a black felt tip pen.

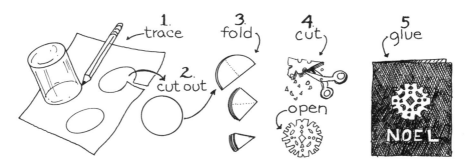

Kaleidoscopes: Use a cup or a glass to draw circles on colorful paper. Cut out the circles. Fold each circle in half, then again in half, and once more in half. Using small nail scissors, cut out little triangles or oval shapes or squares on the edges of the folded circles. When you open them, you will find that each one has an ingenious design a little different from the others. With the palm of your hand, smooth out each circle against a hard flat surface. (You can also put them in a heavy book overnight.) Glue a circle-kaleidoscope in the center of each card. Contrast makes the design even prettier. Put dark-colored designs on light-colored cards; use light-colored designs if you have dark-colored cards.

Typewriter Cards

You can make all kinds of designs by using various letters and signs on the typewriter. The O, V, X, &, ( ), *, and # are especially decorative when typed in interesting patterns. Experiment with your own designs, or use those suggested on these pages. These cards are easy and inexpensive to reproduce on a copying machine if you have many friends and relatives to remember at Christmas, Hanukkah, or other holidays.

MATERIALS: 8¹/₂-by-11-inch typing paper; typewriter; Ko-Rec-Type or Liquid Paper or other correcting substance for errors you may make while typing; felt tip pens.

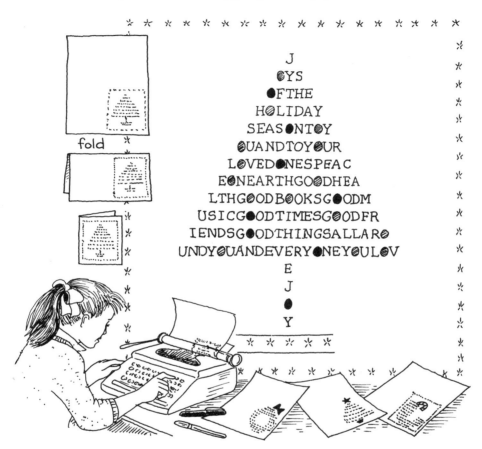

INSTRUCTIONS:

Christmas Tree: Make a typewritten Christmas tree like the one shown here. In the lower right-hand part of the paper, type your holiday message, starting with one letter at the top and continuing (without spaces or punctuation) to the bottom of the tree stand. After the page has been copied in quantity, fold each copy in half, then in half once more, keeping the design on the outside, to fit a 5-by-6-inch baronial envelope. Fill in some of the letters in your message with different colored felt tip pens. Write your name inside the card and add a personal message, if you want to, to anyone who's extra special to you.

Hanukkah Menorah: Follow the diagram for typing a menorah design for Hanukkah cards. Except for the candles and the candle flames, the design is made entirely of typewriter signs: equals, dashes, and parentheses. Draw the outlines of the candles and the flames with a black pen, then make as many copies as you will need to send out to friends and relatives. Decorate the candles with different colored felt tip pens. If you have a yellow highlighter pen, it's perfect for filling in the candle flames, but a yellow or light gold felt tip pen will do fine, too.

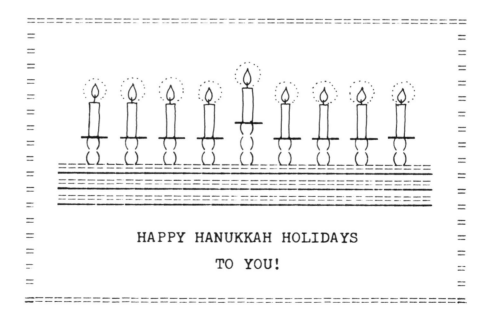

Collage Cards

Many holiday cards can be made by cutting out words, short sentences, or pictures on a single theme from magazines, newspapers, leaflets, etc., and then arranging them in decorative patterns on the front of your card. One New Year's card I've made shows pictures of clocks and watches on the front with a message inside that reads: MAY EACH HOUR OF EVERY DAY BE GOOD NEXT YEAR. Another has a headline reading: SHARE THE GOOD THINGS, with the words FAMILY, JOY, HOLIDAYS, BOOKS, MUSIC, etc., etc., etc., arranged in a pleasing pattern. All of the words come from magazines and newspapers. But these are only suggestions; your own ideas make *your* cards special.

Once you have a design you like, print as many copies as you need at your local copying-machine shop. For a few extra pennies per page, you can have these copies made on colored paper, which is available at most large copying stores. After you fold the cards, you may want to decorate them with stars or other appropriate small stickers. This will take a little time, so plan to spend several days on this project.

MATERIALS: Words, sentences, or pictures from newspapers or magazines; 8½-by-11-inch typewriter paper; stickers; scissors; glue; pen.

INSTRUCTIONS:

Christmas or Other Holiday Cards: Decide on your theme and message and collect words and/or pictures. Arrange them in a pleasing pattern. Glue them to the lower right-hand part of the paper. When the glue is dry, take the paper to a copying machine and make as many copies as you will need to send out.

Fold the pages first in half horizontally and then in half again vertically. The design should be on the outside. Write your name—and personal messages for special people—inside the cards. These will fit into a square envelope.

If you can't find square envelopes in your area, fold the paper twice horizontally; glue your words or pictures to the bottom third as shown. Open the paper up for copying, but after the card is printed, fold the copies so that the picture is on the outside and write your message inside. This size will fit a regular Number 10 business envelope, available anywhere.

Birthday, Anniversary, Graduation, or Other Individual Celebration Cards: Sports, hobbies, and favorite activities all lend themselves to this kind of special card for someone you love. Let's assume that you want to make a birthday card for someone who enjoys music. You could find words that will make a sentence such as: MAY YOUR YEAR BE FILLED WITH MUSIC. Then look for some musical notation in an advertisement or on a piece of old sheet music. (Be sure there is no copyright line on the sheet music. If there is, don't use it or first consult your parent.) Use the music as part of your collage. You could also buy a sheet or two of blank musical notation paper and arrange your words over that. Pay close attention when you look at magazines and newspapers; you will almost always find what you need.

Paste the words or music or pictures on a piece of paper as suggested in the instructions for making holiday cards above. Even if you need only one card, make a copy of it on a copying machine; it will look neater and more "finished" than the original with the pasted-on words.

Photograph Cards

Cards using old or new snapshots can be made for a person's special celebration, such as a birthday, promotion, or retirement. Or you can make them in quantity for holiday sending by having your "creation" copied on a copying machine. The photographs on the copies will not be as sharp and clear as on the original, but they are still handsome and are fun to get during holidays.

Collect old snapshots, with the consent of your family, and be careful not to use pictures that may be precious to someone else. It can be especially nice to use up old pictures on which some people came out looking fine and others look as if they'd just swallowed lemons! (And even sourpuss faces can be perfect for some humorous cards.)

MATERIALS: Old or new snapshots; construction or typing paper or card stock; colored felt tip pen; scissors; glue.

INSTRUCTIONS: Cut out faces, figures, or backgrounds from snapshots. Arrange them in a pleasing pattern—scattered all over the card, grouped in the middle, as a border with a message in the center, etc. When you are satisfied with the design, glue the pictures on card stock or construction paper, if it is to be for one person. Mail it in an appropriately sized manila envelope.

   If the card is to be copied for sending to many people, follow the instructions in *Collage Cards* on pages 11 to 13 for placing, gluing, and copying your photographs. Write your message with a colored felt tip pen inside each card and mail them in 5-by-6-inch baronial envelopes.

Home Printing-Press Cards

This method of printing designs on cards requires things you may not have at home, such as a lino-printing roller and a smoothly edged piece of glass. However, it is worth the cost of buying both at an art supply store, when you realize that store cards are really quite expensive and that you will be able to use the roller and glass for many years.

MATERIALS: Vegetables such as carrots, potatoes, a wedge of cabbage, turnips; leaves, ferns, feathers; textured fabric such as lace, burlap, monk's cloth; string, yarn, or twine; lino-printing roller and glass with smoothly finished edges; watercolor paints; 8½-by-11-inch typing paper or construction paper; knife; large spoon; pen; newspapers.

INSTRUCTIONS:

Shapes and Colors Cards: Spread newspapers on a table or other working surface and on it place your piece of smooth-edged glass. With the roller, spread watercolor paint on top of the glass. Put a piece of clean white paper on another piece of newspaper. Roll the paint-covered roller onto the white paper in different directions. An interesting pattern will emerge. You can add different colors of paint the same way. The mixture of colors can be lovely. Let the paper dry, then fold it with the colorful side out to fit whatever envelopes you have. Write your message inside.

You can vary this procedure by cutting out paper shapes of different kinds: angels, Santas, butterflies, birds, etc. (see the illustration). Roll out paint on top of the glass. Place the paper

shapes on top of the paint on the glass. Put a piece of clean white paper on top of the glass, over the paint and the paper shapes. Press the paper firmly with your hand or with the back of a large spoon. When you lift up the paper, you will find both the background color and the patterns of the shapes transferred to your card. Let the paper dry, fold it, and write your message inside.

Leaf, Feather, and Fabric Prints: Spread newspapers on a working surface. Put the smooth-edged glass on it. Place a pretty leaf, feather, or piece of textured fabric on top of the glass. With the roller, spread paint on the leaf, feather, or fabric. When it is thoroughly saturated with paint, lift it carefully and place it on top of another piece of newspaper. Wash your hands. Put a piece of typing or construction paper over the inked leaf, feather, or fabric and press it with the palm of your hand or with the back of a spoon. Lift up the paper and let it dry. You can repeat this about ten times with one leaf or feather. If you need more cards, take a new leaf, feather, or piece of fabric and repeat the procedure. Let the prints dry, sign them on the back, and send them in large manila envelopes or fold them for mailing in whatever envelopes you have on hand.

Vegetable Prints: Cut a potato, carrot, or turnip in half or cut out a wedge from a head of cabbage. Place the vegetables on the kitchen counter or table and let them air dry for about two hours. Spread newspapers on a working surface. Place the

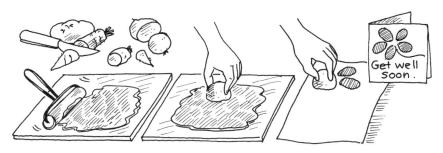

smooth-edged glass and white paper on top of the newspapers. Roll out watercolor paint on the glass. Press the piece of potato, carrot, or other vegetable into the paint, then press it in varied patterns on the white paper. You can vary the ink colors, mix them, alternate the vegetables and mix them, too—do all sorts of interesting things to make your patterns special. Dry the printed paper, then fold it, and sign it.

Pressed Flowers, Ferns, and Grasses Cards

Cards made of pressed flowers are especially lovely for Mother's Day, Father's Day, birthdays, anniversaries, baby births, and other such celebrations. Look on pages 53–54 for names of flowers, ferns, and grasses that are most suitable for drying and for information on how to find out which of these are most available in the area where you live. The flowers most appropriate for drying are also best for pressing.

MATERIALS: Wild flowers, ferns, grasses; flower press (available at most art supply stores or toy shops), or wax paper, aluminum foil, or paper towels and heavy books; construction paper, cards-by-the-pound, or other card stock; glue; scissors; garden shears; newspapers.

INSTRUCTIONS: Cut field flowers, ferns, and grasses. (See page 54.) Spread newspapers on a working surface. If you have a flower press, follow the manufacturer's instructions. If not, spread out your selection of flowers, ferns, and grasses in a single layer between sheets of wax paper, aluminum foil, or paper towels and place them between the pages of a very heavy book. Put the book flat on a bookshelf or table for one to two weeks. (Check after five days or so to make sure the flowers are drying nicely.)

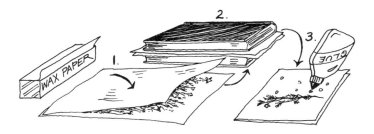

When the flowers are dry, arrange them on a card or piece of construction paper in a pattern that pleases you, or use the illustration as a guide. Handle them gently and carefully. After you have a design you like, put small drops of glue on another card or piece of paper, lift the flowers, and place them gently on top of the glue. Put a clean piece of white paper over the flowers. Smooth them carefully with the palm of your hand, then remove the top piece of paper, and let the glue dry.

Decorations for the Home

$\mathcal{A}$ "Welcome" poster, a colorful wreath on the front door, mobiles moving in the window, or the delicious smell of cinnamon and spices can add to the pleasure of any occasion in your home.

In this section you will find ideas for ways to make your house seem more festive and directions for projects that are quite simple and inexpensive to do.

It doesn't matter what project you choose and whether you use white or purple yarn for a lacy mobile or pinecones or popcorn for a wreath. What matters is that *you* have put in effort, care, and love to help make your home look and feel special.

"Gift Parcel" Door

This decorative door is a welcoming gesture for any holiday or family celebration. It's just as appropriate for a birthday as it is for Thanksgiving. Vary the messages on the tag to suit the occasion.

MATERIALS: Wide, colorful ribbon; measuring tape; posterboard; greenery, or leaves appropriate to holiday and/or season; masking tape or narrow ribbon, string, or yarn; felt tip pen.

INSTRUCTIONS: Measure the height and width of your front door. Double those measurements and add about 70 inches to find the length of wide ribbon you need. Tie the ribbon around the door with a bow in front, as shown in the illustration.

Write a message on a piece of posterboard (about 10 by 14 inches or so), using a pen in a color that matches or contrasts with the color of your door and ribbon. Your message can be corny or clever (YOUR PRESENCE IS A GIFT), simple (WELCOME TO THE LARKINS' THANKSGIVING FEAST), or in keeping with your ethnic background (MI CASA ES SU CASA, which means "My house is your house" in Spanish, or GUT YOM TOV, which means "Happy Holiday" in Yiddish), or whatever you want to say. Attach the posterboard to the door with masking tape, or punch a small hole at the top, slip through a piece of narrow ribbon or string, and tie it to the bow on the door. You could also tuck some greenery into the bow for decoration.

Wreaths

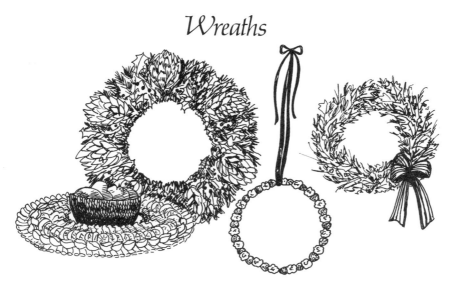

There are many ways of planning and making holiday wreaths. There are also many ways of displaying and using them when they are done. The most common and best known of all wreaths is the evergreen wreath hung on the front door at Christmastime. But lovely wreaths on the front door can welcome guests for other holidays and celebrations. They also can be placed throughout the house or used as dining table centerpieces, with bowls of fruit, flowers, or punch in the middle. And they make nice presents.

Here are some suggestions for a variety of wreaths; or try out other ideas for your very own special creations.

Christmas Wreath

MATERIALS: Styrofoam circle; moss, pinecones, pods, evergreens, holly; ribbon; glue; baskets or bowls; newspapers.

INSTRUCTIONS: Spread newspapers on a working surface. Place all the wreath decorations in baskets or bowls or pile them neatly right on the newspaper. Place the Styrofoam circle on the newspaper and arrange the cones and pods, evergreens and holly on it in different patterns to see which you like best. When you are satisfied with your design, remove the decorations from one quarter of the wreath and spread glue on that part, then place the decorations on top of the glue. Press into place. Let them dry for 10 or 15 minutes before you proceed to the second quarter of the wreath. When you have finished decorating the entire circle, let the wreath dry overnight. The next day, tie a decorative ribbon through the wreath and hang it on the door, or tie a decorative bow and place the wreath on a table.

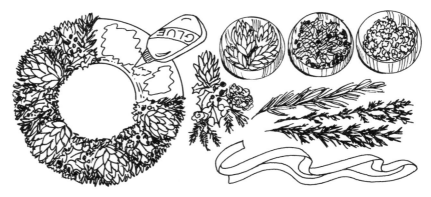

If your wreath is laid on the table, not hung from the door, you can place in it some tiny, light packages, wrapped in Christmas paper and ribbons and containing small gifts like the memo clips, decorative magnets, or other things described on pages 76–83. Tuck the packages in among the greenery and, as guests leave, present each of them with a gift.

Any Holiday Wreath

MATERIALS: Corrugated cardboard from a packing carton; dried or fake flowers, leaves, ferns, etc. (see pages 52–57); decorative fabric, masking tape, or self-adhesive paper; compass; scissors or a single-edged knife; newspapers.

INSTRUCTIONS: Spread newspapers on a working surface. With a compass draw two circles, one within the other, on the corrugated board. The outside circle should be at least 14 or 15 inches in diameter, and the inner circle about 3 or 4 inches smaller. Cut out the ring with strong, sharp scissors or a single-edged knife. Cover it with decorative self-adhesive paper, with colorful masking tape wound around, or with fabric cut to size and glued on. Carefully glue on dried or fake flowers, leaves, and ferns in a pleasing pattern. Let the glue dry and make sure the leaves, etc., are securely attached. (If they don't feel entirely secure, tie them to the wreath with invisible nylon thread for extra support.) Tie a ribbon through the wreath and hang it on the door before any party of the year, or place it on the table for any festive meal, with a small bowl of fruit or nuts, or both, nestled in the middle.

Gumdrops and Popcorn Wreath
MATERIALS: *Popped* corn; gum drops; ribbon; wire.

INSTRUCTIONS: String popcorn and gum drops alternately onto a 30-to-35-inch length of sturdy wire. Shape the wire into a circle and twist the ends together. (If you have trouble forming a wire circle, use a large bowl or platter as a guide.) Tie a ribbon through the wreath and hang it on the door for Halloween, Thanksgiving, Christmas, or any other holiday.

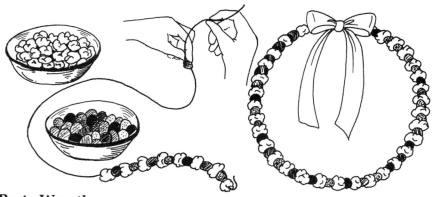

Pasta Wreath
MATERIALS: Assorted shapes of pasta (bow ties, shells, elbows, wagon wheels, etc.); corrugated board, Styrofoam circle, or rim of aluminum-foil pie plate; paint and brush; glue; ribbon; scissors or single-edged knife; newspapers.

INSTRUCTIONS: Spread newspapers on a working surface near an open window or outdoors. Cut a ring out of corrugated board (see directions for *Any Holiday Wreath*, page 23) or use a Styrofoam circle. If you want a very small wreath, you can cut off the rim of an aluminum-foil pie plate and use that as a base. Place the circle on the newspaper and arrange pasta shapes on it in different patterns to see which one pleases you most. When you are satisfied with your design, remove the pasta shapes from one quarter of the circle and spread glue on that part, then place the pasta on top of the glue. Press into place. Let them dry for 10 or 15 minutes before you proceed to the second quarter of the wreath. When you have finished decorating the entire circle, let it dry for about one hour. Paint the wreath in any color suitable for the celebration or season. Or choose a color that looks nice with the tablecloth and napkins, since this wreath is just right for placing on the table with a bowl of flowers or fruit in the middle. If you store this wreath in a box, it can be reused for many special occasions.

Decorated Eggs

At Easter time and on many other special occasions, baskets of decorated eggs look lovely not only on the table where food is served, but anywhere in your house. Egg decoration is an ancient art, and there are many wonderful ways to do it. Here are some very basic, simple suggestions. Choose one of them for your project or make them all!

Basket of Edible Eggs
MATERIALS: Eggs; food coloring; basket; colored tissue paper or napkins; oven mitts or potholders; small paper cups; small paintbrushes; saucepan.

INSTRUCTIONS: Ask your parent how many hard-boiled eggs you will need to serve the expected guests. To prepare them, put the raw eggs in a saucepan with cold water to cover, bring the water to a boil over low heat, and cook for 15 minutes. (Be sure to wear oven mitts or use potholders whenever you cook.) Run the eggs under cold water until they are completely cooled.

Put water in as many paper cups as you have food colors. Add food coloring to each cup until the colors are as dark as you want. Using small paintbrushes, paint the hard-boiled eggs with designs you like or follow the suggestions shown here. Let the eggs dry. Line a straw basket with colored tissue paper or napkins and place the eggs inside. These are both pretty and good to eat, so you can serve them at Easter breakfast or lunch or for any family celebration.

Decorated Natural-Dye Eggs

MATERIALS: Eggs; onion skins, beets or beet peelings, spinach, tomatoes, orange and/or lemon peel; slotted spoon; plate; oven mitts or potholders; fine-point felt tip pens, straight pin, or needle.

INSTRUCTIONS: Ask your parents to save onion skins until you have about four cups full. (You may also have to ask friends and/or neighbors if you can't collect enough in your household.) Fill a large saucepan about three quarters full of water. Add the onion skins and six to nine raw eggs. Using oven mitts or potholders, put the saucepan on the stove over medium heat. Bring the water to a boil, lower the heat, and let the eggs simmer in the onion skins for about 45 minutes. Using oven mitts or potholders, take the eggs out with a slotted spoon and put them on a plate to cool. Since onion skins vary in intensity, the color of your eggs may be light brown, light orange, golden yellow, or many other shades in between.

Other colors can be created by boiling eggs with beets or beet peelings, with spinach or tomatoes, with orange and/or lemon peel, and other fruit and vegetables. You really can't tell ahead of time exactly what shade your eggs will be. The intensity of the colors will vary according to the quantity and kind of vegetables or fruit you use.

Using fine-point felt tip pens, in as many colors as you have or can afford to buy, draw designs on the colored eggs, using the illustrations here as a guide or making up your own. You can also scratch designs on the shells, after they have been dyed, using a needle or straight pin. (Be careful not to scratch designs on your fingers. Just on the egg shells!) Follow the designs here or make up your own. They will show up as white lines against the colored background.

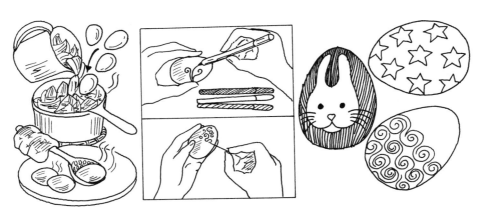

Glittering "Giving Plate"

This plate is nice to hang either on the outside or the inside of the front door when company is expected; guests can take a candy stick as they leave your family party. If you have time, and enough materials, construct several and hang them throughout the house.

MATERIALS: Aluminum-foil pie plates; greenery, leaves, artificial flowers, etc.; candy sticks, licorice straws, peppermint candy canes, etc.; scissors or sharp single-edged knife; glue; hole puncher or screwdriver.

INSTRUCTIONS: Cut one pie plate in half with sturdy scissors or with a single-edged knife. (If you use a single-edged knife, put the plate on a layer of newspapers, with the inside of the plate facing the paper. Hold it by its edge with one hand and cut it away from yourself with the other.) Put the half plate over a whole plate as shown and glue the edges together to make a

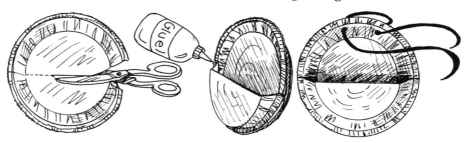

pocket. Punch two holes, about two inches apart, on the whole plate and pull a ribbon or yarn through the holes. Tie the ends. Place greenery and candy inside the pocket and hang the plate wherever you decide.

Vary the greenery or flowers and the candy according to the holiday and season—put in holly and evergreens with peppermint sticks for Christmas; fall leaves and licorice sticks for Halloween; artificial flowers (see pages 52, 55, 56) and red candy sticks for Valentine's Day, etc.

Star of David Mobile

The six-pointed Star of David is a symbolic decoration in many Jewish homes. The decoration suggested here will look festive when hung in a window, from a ceiling light fixture, over a mirror, or on a door.

MATERIALS: Aluminum-foil pie plate; ribbon, yarn, or thread; felt tip pens; scissors; hole puncher.

INSTRUCTIONS: Cut off the rippled edge of the pie plate. Draw a Star of David, as shown in the illustration, on the foil circle. Cut out the star. Color it with felt tip pens on both sides. In the middle of the star you can write SHALOM, which means "peace" in Hebrew. Punch a hole in the top point of the star and pull through a ribbon or thread, tie the ends, and hang the star wherever you like in your house.

Lacy Mobiles

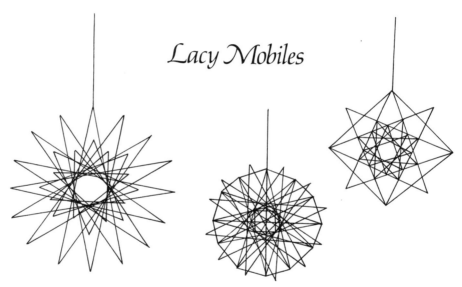

These ornaments look especially nice when hung from curtain rods, ceiling lamps, or hanging plants. Any air movement starts them turning, and they add a festive touch to a party.

MATERIALS: Piece of scrap wood (or a no-longer-used bread-board or chopping block); white embroidery or crochet yarn; small drill (if your parent has one and you have permission to use it) or hammer; rustproof nails; white glue; three bowls of different sizes, or compass; measuring tape; pencil; small mixing bowl; nylon thread; newspapers.

INSTRUCTIONS: Spread newspapers on a working surface. On the piece of wood, draw three circles within one another, using bowls of different sizes or a compass as a guide. Measure—and mark with a pencil—places about one inch apart on each of the three circles. Make small holes, either with nail and hammer or with a small drill, on the marked spots. Hammer a small rustproof nail into each of the holes. Mix one third cup of water with one half cup of white glue in a small bowl. Dip the yarn into the glue, then wind it around the nails in patterns suggested by the illustration, or in any other way you like. When the yarn is completely dry, remove the nails and lift the dry, stiff yarn. Pull a piece of clear nylon thread through one of the points, tie it together, and hang your mobile. You can make as many mobiles as you like by rehammering the nails into the holes and repeating the steps above.

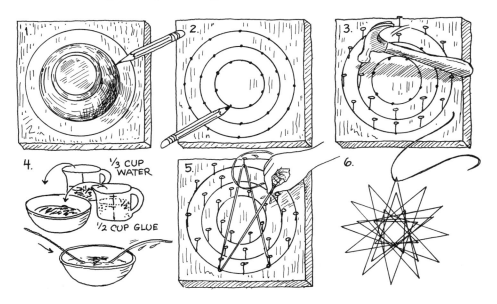

Card Display Mobile

It's fun to display not only Christmas cards, but also the cards that are received for birthdays, confirmations, graduations, new baby in the family, etc. This card display mobile can be decorated to suit whatever occasion is being celebrated—holly and other greenery for Christmas; balloons, streamers, hearts, or flowers for other days. Vary the color of the ribbons from which the cards are suspended according to the celebrations, as well — green and red for Christmas, pink and blue for a baby's birth, etc.

MATERIALS: Small child's umbrella; colorful masking tape; holly, balloons, streamers, cardboard hearts, fake flowers; greeting cards; ribbons; hole puncher; scissors; heavy-duty suction cup hook.

INSTRUCTIONS: Open the umbrella and cut away the fabric. Wind colorful masking tape around the ribs of the umbrella. (Be careful not to poke yourself with a rib while you work.) Tie holly, balloons, streamers, hearts, or flowers — according to the occasion—to the ribs. Punch holes in greeting cards and pull ribbons of varying lengths through the holes. Tie the cards to the ribs of the umbrella among the decorations. Hang the umbrella upside down from a strong suction cup hook on the ceiling or from a hanging light fixture. If your ceilings are very high, you may need to tie a ribbon to the handle of the umbrella and hang the mobile by the ribbon rather than by the handle itself. (An adult's help may be useful when you hang this.)

Mirror Greeting

MATERIALS: Glass wax cleaner; small rag or cotton glove; cotton swabs; small paintbrush.

INSTRUCTIONS: Before a party, write holiday or other celebration-type messages on mirrors throughout the house. Dip a small rag or a cotton-gloved finger in Glass Wax cleaner and write messages such as: HAPPY NEW YEAR, or MIRROR, MIRROR ON THE WALL, WHO'S THE SMARTEST (OR THE FAIREST) OF THEM ALL? and the name of the birthday celebrant or graduate, or CONGRATULATIONS TO GRANDMA AND GRANDPA ON THEIR 35TH WEDDING ANNIVERSARY, or TO MOM ON HER PROMOTION. To make your message more decorative, draw a few hearts and daisies around it with Q-tips or a small paintbrush.

When the party is over, all you have to do is wipe off the wax. You will have not only a pleasant memory of the party, but a sparklingly clean mirror as well!

"All About Adam or Eve" Poster

This is especially appropriate for a special birthday, graduation, or confirmation party. At least a week before the party, ask the friends and relatives of the guest of honor—Adam or Eve or Betty or Joseph—for snapshots, ribbons, medals, or prizes that the honoree may have won, and for other meaningful mementos. Request that the photos show different times in that person's life—from babyhood until the time of the party. Once you have the photos and other materials, you can decide on the theme of your special poster.

MATERIALS: Bulletin board or heavy posterboard; photographs, ribbons, medals, prizes; colored paper; double-faced tape or thumb tacks; felt tip pen.

INSTRUCTIONS: Study the photographs and other materials you have gathered and decide on the theme and size of your poster. Move the photos around on a table or other working surface until you are satisfied with the design and sequence of pictures. Then, cut colored paper in different shapes. On the pieces of paper, write the most amusing and interesting facts about the person's life that you know. Place an appropriate fact underneath, alongside, or above a picture. (You may want to draw arrows from the written material to the photographs to which they relate, or you could put matching numbers on a photo and a comment.) Tack the photos, prizes, medals, ribbons, and the comments to a bulletin board, or use double-faced tape to attach them to posterboard.

Hang the bulletin board or poster in a highly visible place, such as the middle of the wall in the room where the party is taking place, over the table where the party food is, or in the entrance hall where all the guests are likely to see it as soon as they come in.

Balloons with a Message

Balloons on which you have written special messages are an inexpensive and fun way to help decorate the house for a festive occasion. Buy balloons in appropriate colors and ribbons to complement the balloons, then write whatever seems fitting to congratulate someone or to salute a holiday such as the Fourth of July.

MATERIALS: Balloons; balloon ties; long strings or ribbons; felt tip pens; bicycle pump.

INSTRUCTIONS: Using felt tip pens, write messages and make small drawings on balloons, before or after you inflate them. You can draw a smiling sun for a birthday or an umbrella for a bridal shower, etc. (If you get out of breath when you blow up the balloons, use a bicycle pump to inflate them.) Tie the balloons securely and attach ribbons or strings of varying lengths to them. Tie a bunch of balloons together, making sure that they are not all at the same height. Tie the balloon bouquet to a mirror, a window, or a door. Or rub them lightly together and they will rise to the ceiling and hang suspended as if by magic.

Autograph Animals

MATERIALS: White round, stuffed pillow form (available in dime stores); scraps of felt; indelible felt tip pens; needle and thread; scissors.

INSTRUCTIONS: Draw the eyes, whiskers, and mouth of a cat's face on the pillow. Sew on small triangles of colored felt for the cat's ears. Or draw an imaginary animal's face, which can look like a puppy or possum, tiger or lion. Put the date of the party near the bottom of the animal's face or work it in as part of the animal's features. Place the pillow in the entry hall, the living room, the family room, or even in the yard and put some felt tip pens nearby. Ask guests to sign the pillow as they come in.

When guests leave, there will be a permanent memento of the party for your family to share. And if the party is being given for someone's birthday or other celebration, you can present the pillow as your special gift.

Gift-Sheltering Umbrella

Gifts needn't be piled only under Christmas trees. A colorful large umbrella makes a great shelter for presents. Any special occasion at which you give and get presents is going to be more special with this unusual decoration.

MATERIALS: Large, colored umbrella; ribbons; seals, stickers; felt tip pens; glue; scissors.

INSTRUCTIONS: Open the umbrella and decorate it outside and inside by tying on or gluing on whatever you have—seals, stickers, bows, artificial flowers (see pages 52–57), etc. Or paint designs on it with felt tip pens. Place the umbrella in the corner of the room where the party is to be held and put gifts under it.

"Decorated" Houseplants

MATERIALS: Ribbons, tinsel, Christmas decorations; Valentine hearts; small flags; small paper umbrellas; paper stars and hearts; other decorations.

INSTRUCTIONS: You can decorate your houseplants for whatever holiday or celebration is coming up.

1. On Valentine's Day, place paper or foil hearts among the leaves of a plant and *lightly* drape some pink and red ribbons over the leaves and the pot.

2. For Christmas, put tinsel, Christmas balls, etc., among the leaves, especially on large plants that stand on the floor.

3. For a bridal or baby shower, buy some of the very inexpensive paper umbrellas sold in notion stores or in good stationery shops, tuck them in and around a plant, and place the plant on a table near the entry door or where the food is served.

4. For any occasion, decorate houseplant pots with colorful bows and ribbons or place them in colorful gift bags, either

bought or made by you. (To make a gift bag, decorate a brown paper bag with designs cut from colored paper or magazine ads and pasted on, or draw designs directly on the bag with colored felt tip pens.)

Nice Smells for the House

MATERIALS: Cloves, cinnamon sticks, allspice, nutmeg, ginger; saucepan; oven mitts or potholders.

INSTRUCTIONS: An hour or so before your family expects guests, fill a saucepan half-full with water. Add about ten cloves, a cinnamon stick or a teaspoon of powdered cinnamon, and one teaspoon each of nutmeg, allspice, and ginger. (If you don't have all of these spices, use whichever of them you do have and increase the amounts accordingly.) Using oven mitts or potholders, light the stove and place the saucepan over medium heat. Bring the water to a boil, then reduce the heat and let it simmer for about 45 minutes. Turn off the flame but leave the saucepan on the stove until it is completely cool. Your house will smell as if someone had baked all day!

Gift Basket

MATERIALS: Plastic laundry basket; ribbons of all colors and lengths; glue; scissors.

INSTRUCTIONS: Weave colorful ribbons through the hole of a plastic laundry basket. If you need longer ribbons, glue the ends of two ribbons together and let the glue dry before you continue. When you have finished, glue the ends of the ribbons to the outside bottom of the basket. Place the basket in the corner of the room to hold gifts during a children's birthday party or other family celebration.

Table Decorations

The way a table looks at a buffet party, sit-down dinner, or even at a family-only supper when you are celebrating your mom's promotion is important. The most elaborately prepared food just doesn't look as nice or taste as delicious if it isn't served on a nicely set table. And a simple meal of meat loaf and baked potatoes or a vegetarian lasagna can feel like a royal feast if you've folded the napkins in a new and unusual way, placed a small wreath and a bowl of apples in the middle of the table, or arranged some fake flowers made from tissue paper by each plate.

Here, then, are suggestions for decorating and setting a table and making centerpieces, flowers, and other festive things. Before you start, match up the ideas in this section with the kind of special event you are celebrating and compare the materials called for in the various projects with what you have on hand.

Helping to make a table look special is a real joy. It can also bring you lots of compliments from family and friends!

About Centerpieces

In addition to the directions in this section for making specific centerpieces, here are some ways to help liven up a party table with things you probably have on hand or can get easily.

An interesting toy surrounded with a circle of lollipops is a fine centerpiece for a children's party or a baby shower. Each of the guests can take a lollipop home.

A piece of sculpture, decorative small screen, or other art object from your family's shelves, placed on the table and perhaps surrounded by leaves or flowers, can make your table look special.

Inexpensive paper decorations (little umbrellas, flags, chicks, birds, etc.) placed among fruits, nuts, candy, or flowers can reflect the theme of the holiday you are marking.

Gourds, pumpkins, fruits, and vegetables are appropriate decorations for Sukkoth, Thanksgiving, and other fall holidays. Arrange them in a bowl or basket, on a board or tray. A cornucopia-shaped basket is an especially nice container, if you have one. You can make a simple cornucopia from a piece of construction paper, too.

Wreaths of all kinds, some of which are described on pages 21–25 in this book, are lovely as centerpieces, especially if you place a vase or basket with flowers or a bowl with nuts and fruit in the middle of the wreath.

Candles, with or without fresh flowers and fruit, make any table look festive. *But never, never, never put lighted candles near dried or artificial flowers.*

Mug Stand Centerpiece

This makes an especially good centerpiece for a buffet table because it is fairly tall and is visible even if the table is piled with food. If you don't own a mug stand, perhaps you can borrow one or buy one in a dime or hardware store. Mug stands are inexpensive, come in different colors, and hold four to six mugs.

MATERIALS: Mug stand; 3- or 5-ounce paper cups; colorful stickers, self-adhesive paper, or wrapping paper; ribbon, yarn, or wire; glue; fresh or artificial flowers; florists' foam or crumpled tissue paper; hole puncher.

INSTRUCTIONS: Punch holes at opposite sides of four or six paper cups (however many your mug stand holds). If the cups are colorful, you need not decorate them. If they are plain white or just plain dull, paste on decorative stickers for whatever special holiday or occasion you are celebrating: hearts for birthdays, anniversaries, Valentine's Day; eggs or bunnies for Easter; flags for the Fourth of July and other national celebrations, etc. You can also decorate the cups with designs cut out from self-adhesive paper or by gluing on colorful paper from magazines, wrapping paper, etc. Thread a ribbon, yarn, or wire, about 6 to 7 inches long, through the holes on either side of each cup and tie the ends together.

1. Punch holes.   2. Decorate.   3. Thread and tie ribbons.   4. Add flowers.

Arrange flowers in each cup and try to make each a little different in composition. If you use fresh flowers, cut the stems short and fill the cups three quarters full with cold water. If you use dried or artificial flowers, put some crumpled tissue paper or florists' foam in each cup to secure the flowers. When all the cups are filled with flowers, place the mug stand on the table where it will remain for the party and hang the cups on the stand.

Seashell-Flower Centerpiece

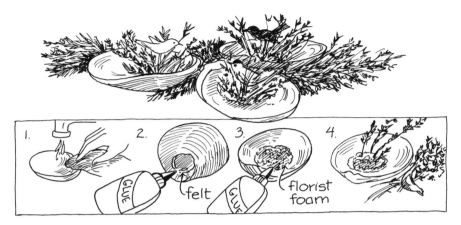

MATERIALS: Good-sized clam shell; dried flowers and grasses; small fake bird from dime store; small piece of felt; florists' foam; glue; newspapers.

INSTRUCTIONS: Clean and wipe the clam shell. Spread newspapers on a working surface. Glue a small piece of felt to the bottom of the shell so it won't scratch the surface on which it will stand. Glue a piece of florists' foam inside the shell. Arrange dried flowers, grasses, and a small bird if you have one, in the foam.

If you have enough shells, make a flower arrangement for each guest. Put each guest's name on a small place card (see page 65) and glue it to a toothpick. Insert the toothpick with the place card amid the flowers and put the seashell at that guest's place at the table. (These make wonderful holiday presents for your guests, as well.)

You can also put three or four such arrangements in the middle of the table and put little cards with gold stars on them inside three or four of the napkins. The lucky people who find the starred cards will get an arrangement at the end of the party!

Sweet Centerpiece

MATERIALS: Foil or paper cupcake liners; jelly beans, candy corn, or hard candy; short, colored pencils or crayons; tray or plate.

INSTRUCTIONS: Place three or four cupcake liners inside one another for strength. Prepare as many cups as there will be guests at the party. Fill each one with candy. Insert a short, clean, sharp pencil or crayon in the middle of each, pointed side up, so it resembles a candle. Place the "candles" on a pretty tray or plate and put it in the middle of the table. This will be not only an unusual and pretty centerpiece, but one that can be given away, cup by cup, to guests at the end of the party.

About Vases and Other Flower Containers

There is nothing prettier or more inviting than flowers on a party table or when your family gathers for a special meal together. In addition to the individual vase projects described later, here are suggestions for vases made or recycled from other containers.

A pretty tin tea box makes a lovely flower container. These are usually so decorative that they don't need any additional work. (The ones from England and other foreign countries are especially nice looking.) A metal container is best used for dried or artificial flowers, since water may leak out or rust the metal.

A cookie tin — round, square, oblong, or tall—is also a fine flower container. Many such tins have boldly printed brand names; you may want to cover these. You can paint the tin (see instructions on page 59) and then decorate it with stickers, glued-on jewelry bits, etc. You can also decorate it like the *Gilded Vase* (see page 50) or the *"Porcupine" Vase* (see page 49). Cookie-tin flower containers usually look best filled with low-stemmed dried or fake flowers, nicely arranged in florists' foam.

Small cans can hold flowers, too. Save cans from juice or soup, fruit or tomato sauce, remove the brand labels, and wash the cans with soap and water several times. When they are dry, decorate them as you would a cookie tin (see above), fill them three quarters full of water, and arrange fresh flowers with short stems in them. You can also fill them with florists' foam and arrange artificial or dried flowers.

Glass jars or juice bottles, well washed, can be decorated in colorful designs with waterproof markers (such as Faber Castell). Or you can paste on cutouts from magazines, old greeting cards, wallpaper, or other pretty paper. Use a waterproof glue such as Duco and coat the paper designs afterward with clear nail polish. For a special effect, glue rickrack or other decorative ribbons around the edges of the jars or bottles with waterproof glue. Then fill them three quarters full of water and arrange fresh flowers in them.

Baskets are pretty containers for dried or artificial flowers. Put florists' foam inside the basket, secure it with tape, and arrange the flowers to suit your whim. Add little paper umbrellas, small fake birds, little flags, or other decorations to make each flower basket special and unique for your party. Even small snapshots of the guest of honor can be tucked among the flowers.

Pitchers of all kinds make wonderful vases, especially for field flowers and dried flowers. Watering cans, with long or short spouts, work well for a large buffet table. You can decorate them or leave them be—whatever your fancy dictates.

Paper towel tubes, toilet paper tubes, oatmeal boxes, and other cardboard containers make fine vases for fake or dried flowers. Cover the cardboard with foil or brightly colored paper and arrange the containers in groups. For instance, you can surround one paper towel tube with several toilet paper tubes, all nicely covered with decorative paper, and tie them together with a colorful ribbon. Use appropriate ribbons for different holidays: red, white, and blue for the Fourth of July; bright green for St. Patrick's Day; orange and black for Halloween. Fake or dried flowers with different length stems can be arranged in these containers very handsomely, and no one will know where the "vase" originated.

Plastic bottles from household cleaners can be decorated as well. Remove the brand labels, wash the bottles thoroughly with soap and water several times, and let them dry. Then paint designs on the bottles, using model kit paints, or decorate them with stickers, stars, colorful paper, cutouts, etc. These bottles are best used with dried and artificial flowers, or with field flowers that have long stems.

"Porcupine" Vase

MATERIALS: Glass jar or bottle; white rice; glue; small brush; paints and brush; newspapers.

INSTRUCTIONS: Remove any paper labels from the jar or bottle. Wash the jar or bottle with soap and water, rinse several times, and dry well. Spread newspapers on a working surface. On one part of the newspaper, spread about two cups of white rice. Spread white glue all over the bottle with a small brush.

Roll the glue-covered bottle or jar in the rice. Let it dry. Brush another coat of glue over the rice on the bottle and roll it again on the loose rice. Let it dry. When the glue is completely dry, dab the bottle with colored paints in free style or follow whatever patterns you like. (If you don't have differently colored paints, you can use nail polish or felt tip pens.)

It's safer to arrange dry or artificial flowers in this vase because water may loosen the rice and make it fall off.

Gilded Vase

MATERIALS: Large juice or coffee can; different shapes of pasta (elbow, corkscrew, shell, bow ties, wagon wheels, etc.); small brush; white glue; paint and brush; newspapers; two bricks or heavy stones.

INSTRUCTIONS: Wash the can with soap and water, remove any paper labels, and dry the can well. Spread newspapers on a working surface, and prop the can between heavy stones or bricks. Arrange different shapes of pasta on the paper until you find a design that appeals to you or follow the pattern on the illustration shown here. Then spread white glue with a brush on part of the can and arrange the pasta in the glue. Let it dry.

1. Spread glue.
2. Add pasta.
3. Repeat until can is covered.

GLUE

4. two coats of paint

Gold

When the pasta on that part of the can is securely glued, move the can gently and prop it up again with the bricks or heavy stones. Glue on more pasta. Repeat until the entire outside of the can has been covered. Put the can upside down on the paper and paint it with gold, silver, or bronze paint until all the pasta and can surface have been covered. Let it dry. Give a second coat of paint and let it dry again.

This vase is good for both fresh and dried flowers. You can also decorate soup, juice, or other small cans in this way and use them as individual flower arrangements at each place setting. Each guest can take one home as a holiday present or party favor.

Yarn Flowers

MATERIALS: Heavy worsted yarn—of different colors, if possible; kitchen rolling pin or vacuum cleaner tube or other round object at least 2 inches in perimeter; scissors; pipe cleaners.

INSTRUCTIONS: Put a piece of heavy worsted yarn, about 10 to 12 inches long, along the length of a kitchen rolling pin or a vacuum cleaner tube or other long, round object. Wind a second piece of yarn, about 60 inches in length, over it as shown in the diagram. After you have made about thirty turns, tie the

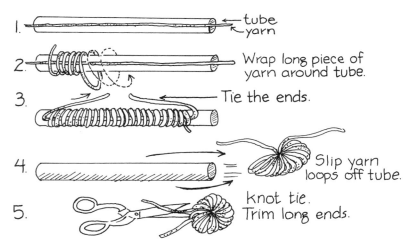

1. ← tube
   ← yarn
2. Wrap long piece of yarn around tube.
3. Tie the ends.
4. Slip yarn loops off tube.
5. knot tie. Trim long ends.

ends of the straight piece of yarn together over the wound yarn. Slip the yarn off the tube. (The yarn will be round and look like a mum or small aster.) Tighten the tie and knot it again. Cut off the ends of the yarn that tied the flower. Repeat until you have eight or ten flowers.

Bend about 2 inches at the end of a pipe cleaner into a small hook and slip this hook through the middle of each flower. Wind the hooked end around the "stem" of the flower, as shown here. Repeat with each of the flowers you have made

6. Bend pipe cleaner. 7. Hook into flower. 8. Wind hook around stem.

until you have a nice bouquet of colored yarn flowers to arrange in a vase. You can add artificial green leaves from the dime store, if you want.

Air-Dried Flowers

Many kinds of field and garden flowers lend themselves to air drying, but the kinds may vary from one geographic area to another. Therefore, it would be helpful to ask an experienced gardener or florist about flowers in your area that will air dry well. Usually good are mums, baby's breath, goldenrod, heather, hydrangea, milkweed, statice, strawflower, and yarrow. These grasses and berries are also fine for air drying: foxtails, millet, oats, wheat, bittersweet, and sumac.

MATERIALS: Field and/or garden flowers; garden clippers; bucket or large jar; rubber bands; clothesline or heavy cord.

INSTRUCTIONS: Cut flowers with garden clippers on a sunny afternoon, after all the dew has evaporated from the earth. While you work, stand the flowers in a bucket or jar filled with cool water so they won't wilt. When you have collected a nice bunch, strip all the foliage from the stem of each flower. Tie about twelve to fourteen stems together with a strong rubber band. Hang them upside down from a clothesline or heavy cord in an attic or garage. If you live in an apartment, this is somewhat harder to handle, but flowers will dry in a dark, dry closet. (Or you can use Silica-Gel to dry flowers. Follow the instructions given on the box; they are easy and clear.)

After a week or two, the flowers should be dry and ready for arrangements. Put florists' foam into your container and arrange the flowers in any way you like.

Felt Flowers

MATERIALS: Yellow, white, and black felt remnants (available in dime stores); florists' wire and tape, or pipe cleaners; white paper and pencil; straight pins; scissors.

INSTRUCTIONS: Draw a daisy pattern on white paper, following the shape shown here. Repeat with the pattern for a black-eyed Susan, also shown here. Cut both out. Pin the daisy pattern to two thicknesses of white felt and the black-eyed Susan pattern to two thicknesses of yellow felt.

Cut around the patterns. To one of each of the shapes, glue a piece of florists' wire or a pipe cleaner. Glue on the matching shape to cover the "stems." Repeat until you have as many flowers as you want. Cut out small black felt circles for the centers of the black-eyed Susans and small yellow circles for the centers of the daisies. Glue one on each side of each flower. Put some florists' foam in a bowl, vase, or container and arrange the flowers. If you like, you can add some fake leaves from the dime store.

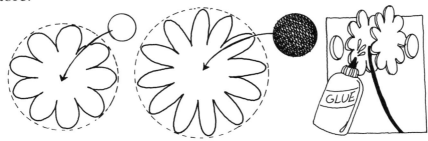

Phantom Roses and Fake Carnations

MATERIALS: White or colored facial tissues; lipstick; pipe cleaners or florists' wire or plastic twist ties; nail scissors.

INSTRUCTIONS: Hold the center of a tissue between your fingers and shake it downward. With your other hand, wind a pipe cleaner, a piece of florists' wire, or a long plastic tie around the center of the tissue just below your fingers. Using nail scissors, cut the corners of the tissue to make rounded petals for phantom roses. For fake carnations, snip the edges of the tissue to make fringelike petals. Holding the stem, turn the tissue upward. Brush the flower petals with lipstick, from about an inch inside the flower to the edge. Brush lightly and freely and don't aim for uniformity on the petals. Let each one look different from the other. The fragrance of the lipstick will give the flowers a pleasant aroma.

Put the flowers in a vase, box, or bowl and add leaves from the dime store to the arrangement if you wish. I prefer these without leaves, for the "blossoms" are very delicate and look just fine by themselves.

Fruit or Vegetable Candle Holders

MATERIALS: Two large apples (such as Rome Beauty or Cortland), oranges, grapefruit, or small pumpkins; candles; fresh flowers; apple corer or sharp knife; skewer or small screwdriver; scissors or garden shears.

INSTRUCTIONS: Select two large fruits or small pumpkins that can stand securely on a plate or directly on the table. Cut out enough of the cores of each so that candles can fit in snugly. Light an old candle and drip some warm wax into each hole. Insert your party candles and press them down in the wax until they feel secure. With a skewer or small screwdriver, poke holes in the fruits or pumpkins. Cut some garden flowers (zinnias, marigolds, mums, etc.) or field flowers (daisies, black-eyed Susans, etc.) with very short stems. (*Never use fake or artificial flowers with candles!*) Insert the flowers into the holes. Place the fruits or pumpkins on a small saucer or plate or directly on the table.

Glass Candlesticks

MATERIALS: Short, clear drinking glasses or glass jars; candles; colorful fish-tank gravel or sand, or pretty marbles, pebbles, shells, or stones.

INSTRUCTIONS: Wash and dry the glasses or jars. Light an old candle and drop a small mound of warm wax into the center of each. Stand your party candle in the warm wax and press until it feels secure. Arrange colorful fish-tank gravel or sand around the candles in each glass or jar. If there's no pet shop nearby where you can buy the gravel or sand, collect pretty stones or shells or pebbles and place them around the candles. Colored marbles also look just dandy.

You can make as many candle holders as you like and put candles of different colors and heights in them. Arrange the holders in the middle of the dining table in a group or spread them the length of the table. You can also place one of these candle holders in the middle of a wreath made of gumdrops and popcorn (see page 24) on a small table in the house. *Never light candles in the middle of a wreath made of dried flowers and ferns.*

Candles and Flowers

MATERIALS: Small soup, juice, or fruit cans; enamel paint; small stones, shells, and pebbles of different shapes and varieties; candles; fresh flowers; two heavy stones and bricks; small brush; glue; newspapers.

INSTRUCTIONS: Wash the cans with soap and water, remove any paper labels, and dry the cans well. Spread newspapers on a working surface near an open window or outdoors. Paint the cans with any color enamel paint that seems suitable for your table. Let the paint dry. Place a can sideways, propping it between heavy stones or bricks. Arrange small shells, pebbles, or stones on the paper until you find a design you like. Spread glue with a brush on part of the can and arrange the pebbles, stones, and shells in the glue. Let dry. Gently turn the can and continue decorating it with more shells and pebbles. When the entire outside of the can is decorated and dry, stand it upright. Light an old candle and drip a small mound of warm wax into the center of the can. Place a *tall* party candle in the wax and press until it stands firmly in place. Fill the can about one half full with water and arrange fresh flowers with fairly short stems around the candle.

About Table Coverings

In addition to the pretty tablecloths your family may already have on hand, here are a few suggestions for table coverings for special occasions, as well as many other simple ways to set a table so that it looks different and lovely.

Lacy paper doilies, round or oblong, look great for a special birthday, Valentine's Day, baby shower, or other family gatherings. They show up especially well if you put them over a dark-colored table or tablecloth, or over brightly colored pieces of felt or other fabric. Cleanup time will be easy—the doilies can be discarded when the party is over.

Bandanas make good table mats, especially blue and red ones for a Fourth of July party. Place them on the table in diamond fashion under the plates, with one corner hanging down over the edge of the table and the other three corners on top of the table, as shown in the diagram.

Dish and hand towels in simple or colorful patterns are pleasant on an informal or children's party table. If they are large enough, arrange them on the diagonal, across the width of the table, and set two place settings on each towel. Smaller ones are just right for one person.

Odd lengths of patterned fabric left over from family projects make fine table coverings. If they are small, about 12 by 15 inches, hem or fringe them and use them as mats. If they are longer, use them as runners down the length and width of the table. Look at the diagrams here; you will get an idea of how odd lengths of fabric can be used to set a table.

 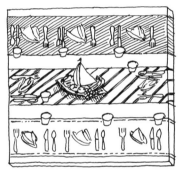 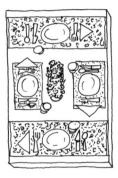

Colorful bed sheets make terrific tablecloths. They are easy to wash, are big enough for even large picnic tables, can be folded to smaller size for indoor tables, and come in all kinds of patterns. If you don't have any spare sheets at home, ask if you can buy one when sheets are on sale. A flat twin-size sheet can be quite inexpensive, and it will last for years.

You can also use plain white sheets and decorate them with waterproof fabric dye markers (those by Delta are especially good) in designs to suit your taste and the special celebration. Write messages of holiday cheer or congratulation and decorate them by drawing pictures of pumpkins and broomsticks for Halloween, Christmas bells and angels for Christmas, etc.

Beach towels in bright, bold colors and patterns make wonderful outdoor tablecloths. They are heavy enough so that the wind won't sweep them off the table, they absorb spills and hardly ever show stains, and they look well with all kinds of colorful napkins.

Place Mats

MATERIALS: Cardboard, or old plastic mats; old greeting cards, scraps of wallpaper, magazine ads, etc.; glue; clear self-adhesive paper; scissors; newspapers.

INSTRUCTIONS: Cut cardboard into as many 11-by-14 inch pieces as you will have guests. (Or use old plastic mats.) Spread newspapers on a working surface. Cut out pictures or designs you like from greeting cards, magazine pages, wallpaper, etc. Arrange them in pleasing patterns on the mats. After you are satisfied with the designs, glue the pictures down and let them dry. Cut a piece of clear self-adhesive paper, 13 by 16 inches, for each mat. Put the paper on the newspaper with the backing side up. Peel the backing off and carefully and slowly place your mat, picture side down, in the center of the clear paper, leaving

1. Cut out pictures.

11"

cardboard or old plastic place mat

14"

2. Glue pictures to mat.

3. Stick mat to self-adhesive paper.

13"

16"

picture side down

4. To miter: Cut off paper corners. Fold up sides.

an overlap on each side. Miter the corners as shown in the diagram. Bring up the edges of the paper and press them to the back of the mat.

These mats will be colorful and easy to clean. To make them extra special, cover all or some with pictures of things each person at your table likes. For example, if your brother loves tennis or your sister is crazy about hockey, use pictures of these sports. Thoughtfulness like this makes any meal memorable.

Signature Tablecloth

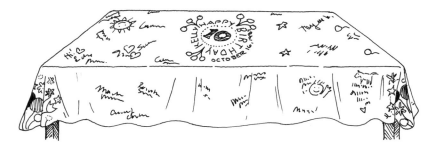

MATERIALS: Muslin by the yard or solid-colored bed sheet; indelible fabric dye markers (Delta is good); needle and thread; scissors.

INSTRUCTIONS: Buy two and one-half yards of muslin and hem it, or use a white or solid-colored flat twin-size sheet. With fabric dye markers, draw corner designs and a center picture as indicated in the illustration here.

If the tablecloth is for a special occasion such as a birthday, anniversary, graduation, shower, new baby, etc., write the date and reason for the celebration in big, bold letters either in one corner or in the center. As each guest arrives, ask him or her to sign the tablecloth and write whatever greeting he or she likes. The tablecloth will be a special keepsake for the person in whose honor the party is being held.

If it is a family gathering for a holiday such as Hanukkah or Easter, have guests write a message, sign it, and date it. This tablecloth can be used for years and years on the same holiday, with new signatures and dates added each year. It will become an "heirloom" and a reminder of special times in your family.

Place Cards

Decorated Cards

MATERIALS: Card stock or unlined index cards; scraps of self-adhesive paper or colorful decals or fabric; scissors; glue; felt tip pens.

INSTRUCTIONS: Cut card stock into 4-by-6-inch pieces, or use 3-by-5-inch unlined index cards. Fold in half lengthwise. Write the name of each guest on the outside of a card and stand it by the place setting where he or she will sit. You can decorate the place cards with felt tip pen dots or borders or little flowers or smiling faces or whatever suits your fancy. If you don't feel "artistic" enough to draw, paste on pretty decals or cut out a design from colorful paper or fabric and glue it to the place card.

   The decorated cards can be used as gift tags, too.

Recycled Cards

MATERIALS: Old greeting cards; scissors; glue; self-adhesive labels; colorful pen.

INSTRUCTIONS: Recycle pretty greeting cards by making them into place cards. Cut a section about 4 by 6 inches out of the prettiest or most interesting part of a card (make sure there is no writing on the other side) and fold it in half. Write the name of the guest on a small self-adhesive label and paste it in the center of the top part of the card.

About Table Settings

If you are asked to help set the table for a festive meal, your parent surely will tell you what kind of dishes and silverware you should set out and how these should be arranged on the table. There are different ways to set a table, depending on how many courses there will be, how the food is to be served, etc. (You can look these up in an illustrated cookbook or in magazines that feature food, if you are curious.)

But for family celebrations, especially if you are setting the table by yourself, here are some very basic guidelines and diagrams to help you.

A sit-down dinner or lunch usually calls for these dishes at each place: a dinner plate, a bread and butter or salad plate, and a water glass. If soup or an appetizer will be served, those plates are usually brought to the table with the food already in them. Dessert plates and cups and saucers are also brought later, after the other plates have been cleared from the table.

The following silverware is usually part of the table setting: a meat fork, salad or dessert fork, knife, soup spoon (if needed), and teaspoon. Look at the diagrams for proper placement of dishes and silverware at the start of a meal.

AMERICAN SETTING

SMALL FORK (SALAD OR DESSERT)
LARGE FORK (MAIN COURSE)
PLATE AND/OR NAPKIN
GLASS
KNIFE
DESSERT OR COFFEE SPOON
SOUP SPOON

EUROPEAN SETTING

NAPKIN HERE OR ON PLATE OR NEXT TO KNIFE
SMALL FORK
LARGE FORK
PLATE
SOUP AND DESSERT SPOONS
KNIFE
GLASS

A buffet meal usually calls for a dinner plate, dessert plate, mug or cup and saucer, and a water glass; a meat fork, knife, teaspoon, and dessert fork or spoon. These can be arranged in any way that is convenient for people to pick them up, or you can follow the diagram shown here.

Flowers, pretty centerpieces, candles, place cards, unusually folded napkins—any of these can help to make the table look especially attractive.

Napkin Folding

You can buy paper napkins made especially for Christmas and Halloween, St. Patrick's Day and Thanksgiving, for graduations, anniversaries, and other celebrations at almost all stationery stores and supermarkets. But pretty napkins without greetings also come in many colors, patterns, and sizes, in paper or cloth, and they can make the table look as colorful as you like. By folding them in unusual ways, you can add your own special contribution to the way a table looks.

Here are some ideas for napkin arrangements for you to try. A little practice before a party will result in a better-looking table when guests arrive. Sometimes paper napkins lend themselves to certain folding patterns more easily than cloth napkins do, and cloth napkins look nicer in others. The directions below point out which kind is best for which.

Candles in Glass: Fold a cloth napkin in half. Roll it diagonally, as shown in the diagram. When completely rolled, fold the napkin in half again and put it in a water glass. (Use a tall glass if the napkin is large or a short one if the napkin is medium sized.) The open ends of the napkin should face up. A very sturdy paper napkin can also be rolled this way, but it will crease and won't look as nice as a cloth napkin when it is unrolled later.

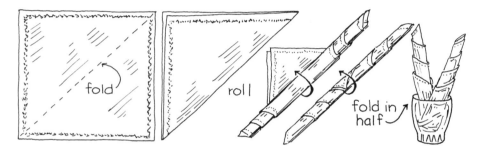

Boat: Fold a cloth or sturdy paper napkin in half and then in half again, as shown in the diagram. Then fold it on the diagonal, as shown, and turn up a small rim on both sides. Stand the napkin boat near a place setting and let it "sail" with your party.

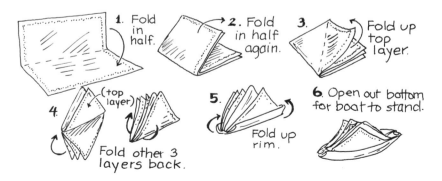

Bird in Flight: Fold a regular paper napkin in half and then in half again, as shown in the diagram. Then fold it on the diagonal. Insert the diagonal side of the napkin between the prongs of a fork, as shown. Press the triangle end of the napkin into a bird's beak. Put the napkin birds on top of dinner or lunch plates or arrange them on a buffet table between the knives and spoons.

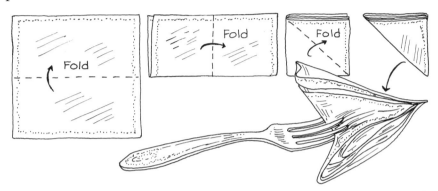

Silverware Pocket: Fold a cloth or sturdy paper napkin in half and then in half again, as shown in the diagram. Roll down one layer in a cloth napkin, or three layers in a paper napkin, as shown. Fold the two sides to the back. Put a fork, knife, and spoon in the pocket and place the napkin near a dinner or lunch plate, or on the buffet table.

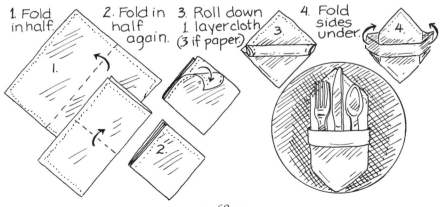

Fan: Fold a sturdy paper napkin in half. Make accordion pleats all the way to the top. Put the napkin halfway into a tall or medium-height glass and let the top open up, as shown in the diagram.

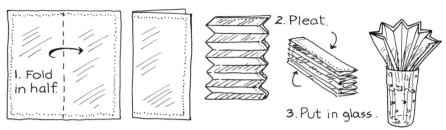

Pinwheel: Bring the top and bottom of a sturdy paper napkin to the center. Fold the napkin in accordion pleats, as shown in the diagram. Holding one end, spread out the pleats; the napkin will look like a pinwheel. (You can put a *Memo Clip*, see page 78, in the middle.) Put a napkin on top of each plate on a dinner table or arrange several in a row on a buffet table.

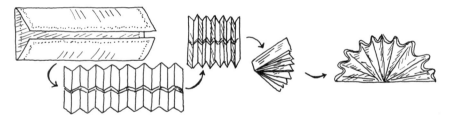

Gift Holder: Fold a paper napkin in half and then in half again, as shown in the diagram. Fold three corners to the center and turn the napkin over. Fold the top flap down. Put a small gift or surprise in the center and place the napkin on the dinner or buffet table.

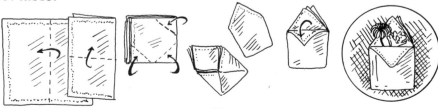

Napkin Rings

MATERIALS: Paper towel or aluminum-foil tube; colorful paper and glue or self-adhesive paper; sharp knife or single-edged blade; newspapers.

INSTRUCTIONS: Spread newspapers on a working surface. Cut the tube into six 2-inch circles. Cover each circle with colorful self-adhesive paper or glue on bright paper. Roll a paper or cloth napkin, slip it through a ring, and put it at each place on your table.

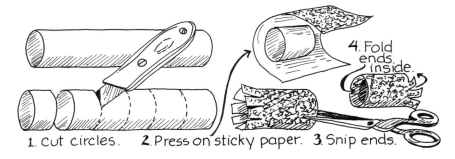

1. Cut circles.　2. Press on sticky paper.　3. Snip ends.

These napkin rings can be re-used many times, of course, or they can be specially decorated for an individual holiday and used only on those days year after year. For a special holiday, decorate the rings with flags for the Fourth of July, pictures of four-leaf clovers or shamrocks for St. Patrick's Day, pictures of Hanukkah candles, etc.

Napkin Holders

Wire Holder

MATERIALS: Colored wire coat hanger, or regular wire hanger and colored masking tape.

INSTRUCTIONS: Twist the coat hanger as shown in the illustration. If the hanger is made of plain wire, cover it with masking tape. This holder is handy for outdoor parties and will hold a large number of big napkins quite securely.

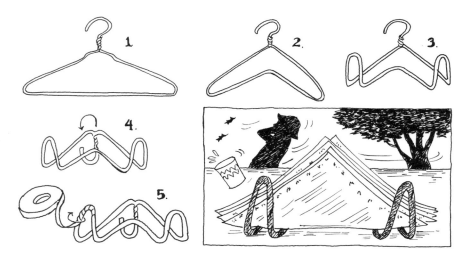

Decorated Holder

MATERIALS: Two large, sturdy paper plates; decorative stickers, photographs, or pictures from magazines; scissors; glue.

INSTRUCTIONS: Cut a 2-to-3-inch strip from the middle of one paper plate. Decorate one side of the strip with stickers or glue on pictures from pretty magazine ads or photographs. Glue the edges of the strip to the middle of the second plate,

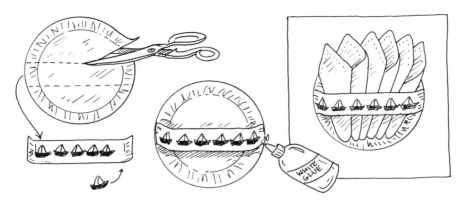

picture side up, as shown. Fold napkins in half or in thirds, or however you wish, and slip them under the band. It will keep the napkins from flying away at an outdoor party.

Personalized Glasses

MATERIALS: Plastic party glasses; felt tip pens or Faber Castell markers.

INSTRUCTIONS: Use colorful pens or markers to decorate as many glasses as there will be guests at your party, following the patterns shown here or making up any design you like. (Since

Faber Castell markers work particularly well on plastic, you may want to buy some. But try your regular felt tip pens first and see how the writing "sticks" to the plastic.) When you write a guest's name on a glass, add a decorative doodad or two and let the guest take his or her glass home when the party is over.

You can put a fancily folded napkin (see pages 67–70) in each glass before you place it on the table.

Coasters

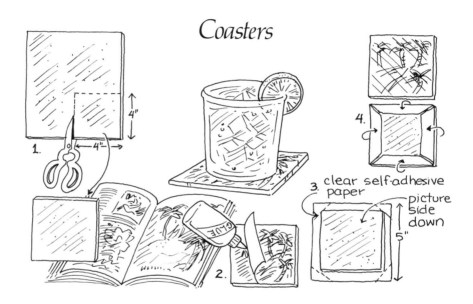

MATERIALS: Heavy cardboard; colorful magazine pictures, snapshots, or decorative paper; clear self-adhesive paper; glue; knife or single-edged razor blade or scissors; ruler; newspapers.

INSTRUCTIONS: On the cardboard, draw a 4-by-4-inch square for each coaster you want to make. Cut out the squares with a strong scissors or put the cardboard on a thick layer of newspapers on your working surface and cut carefully with a single-edged razor blade. Using the cardboard squares as a size guide, cut out interesting pictures from magazines or from old duplicate snapshots. Glue them to one side of the cardboard squares. Cut a piece of clear self-adhesive paper, 5 by 5 inches, for each coaster. Put the paper on the newspaper with the backing side up. Peel the backing off and carefully and slowly place each coaster, picture side down, in the center of the clear paper, leaving an overlap on each side. Miter the corners as shown on page 63. Bring up the edges of the paper and press them to the back of the coaster.

These coasters also make nice small wall pictures, and they can be given away as favors at the end of your party. To hang them as pictures, attach a small ribbon or wire loop to the back of each coaster with masking tape.

Party Favors, Small Presents, and Gifts of Time

On the following pages you will find some ideas for making small gifts and favors that you can present to your friends and relatives at parties and holiday celebrations. Some of them are so decorative that they also can be used to brighten the dinner or buffet table. By the same token, many of the home and table decorations described earlier in this book—wreaths, vases, arrangements of dried or fake flowers, mobiles, coasters—make good party favors as well.

There are also suggestions here for "gifts of time," which happen to be my favorite presents to give and to receive. These are memorable gifts not only for holidays and particular occasions, but throughout the entire year, and they only need your time and goodwill and care to make them special.

No recipes for candy or cookies or other treats of food are included in this section of party favors, but homemade food is always a welcome gift. You can find good recipes in holiday cookbooks and in magazines or newspapers.

Homemade candy is particularly nice to give after a party. You can put the candy in clear plastic bags and tie them with gay ribbons, then put the packages in a basket on the party table or by the door and give them out to the guests as they are leaving.

Soft cookies that won't crumble also make fine favors. Put them in small brown paper bags, decorate the bags with felt tip pens or colorful stickers, tie them with colorful ribbons, and line them up on a shelf by the door or on the holiday table.

Paperweights

MATERIALS: Medium-sized smooth stones; enamel paints and brush; clear nail polish; newspapers.

INSTRUCTIONS: Wash the stones and dry them in the sun or near a radiator or stove. Spread newspapers on a working surface. Paint a design you like on the stones or follow the patterns shown here. (You could paint an entire stone a solid color and let it dry, then paint a design in other colors.) When all the painting is done, let the stones dry overnight. Then cover the designs or the entire stones with clear nail polish. Let the stones dry again. If your stones aren't smooth, glue a small piece of felt on one side of each stone. This will prevent scratches on tables or desk surfaces.

These stones make terrific napkin weights at outdoor parties as well as nice party favors. If you like, write the name of the gift recipient and sign your name and date on the stone as well.

Bookmarks

MATERIALS: Metal hair clips; felt remnants; glue; scissors; newspapers.

INSTRUCTIONS: Spread newspapers on a working surface. Cut pieces of felt big enough to cover a whole hair clip or cut out designs like those suggested in the illustration. Glue the felt to the tops of the hair clips. This gift will keep the place in books read by your friends and relatives.

If you like, you can put place cards in the clips and clip them to the napkins or set them at each guest's plate.

Memo Clips

MATERIALS: Wooden spring-type clothespins; enamel paint and brush; beads, buttons, small pebbles, or seashells; ribbon, small stickers, etc.; glue; newspapers.

INSTRUCTIONS: Spread newspapers on a working surface. Paint the clothespins carefully on all sides. Let them dry. Arrange buttons, beads, pebbles, or small seashells in a pattern you like on the surfaces of the clothespins. When you are satisfied with how they look, glue them on. Do not glue them to the parts of the clothespin that you press to open; they will fall off after a few openings and closings. Either leave those ends plain or decorate them with stickers, bits of decorative paper, or ribbons.

These clips are nice for holding notes or memos by the telephone, on a desk, etc. Or you can buy small note pads in the stationery or dime store, write a guest's name on the first page of each pad, and put one in each memo clip. These can serve as place cards for dinner as well as useful and good-looking favors for guests to take home afterward. The clips also make excellent paper napkin holders, especially outdoors.

Clipboards

MATERIALS: Pieces of plywood or heavy cardboard, about 8½ by 11 or 5 by 7 inches; self-adhesive paper, fabric, or decorative paper; metal clips (Number 2 for larger-size boards, Number 1 for smaller boards), available at stationery, hardware, or dime stores; scissors; glue; newspapers.

INSTRUCTIONS: Spread newspapers on a working surface. Cover both sides of the plywood or cardboard with self-adhesive paper or glue on fabric or decorative paper. Clip the metal clip to one end of the board. Slip a piece of paper under the clip and write a cheerful message for the recipient of this useful gift.

Decorative Magnets

MATERIALS: Inexpensive metal or plastic magnets from the notions or hardware store; scraps of felt, buttons, small seashells, "junk" jewelry; glue; scissors; newspapers.

INSTRUCTIONS: Spread newspapers on a working surface. Glue to the top of each of the magnets a pretty piece of "junk" jewelry or a button or a seashell. Or cut out interesting shapes from felt—hearts, apples, berries, or whatever seems pretty—and glue them on.

You can make the magnets even more special by decorating them to suit the holiday when you will give them as party favors—glue on red felt hearts for Valentine's Day, green trees for Christmas, or orange pumpkins or red apples for Thanksgiving.

Pomander Balls

MATERIALS: Oranges, lemons, limes or grapefruit; whole cloves; powdered cinnamon, ginger, allspice, nutmeg; bowls; cookie sheet; ribbon.

INSTRUCTIONS: Stick whole cloves into the skin of the fruit, covering the surface as closely as possible. (Don't worry if some cloves break off. Just collect them in a bowl or bag and use them when you make *Nice Smells for the House*, page 39.) In a bowl, mix cinnamon, ginger, allspice, and nutmeg. The amount you will need depends on what fruit you are using and how many pomander balls you are making. Roll the clove-studded fruit in the spice mixture. Shake off any excess into the bowl. Set the fruit on a cookie sheet and let it air-dry for about 24 hours. Tie each fruit with a ribbon, as shown.

Pomander balls make wonderful presents, as well as fine decorations for your own home. They can be hung in a closet or from a light fixture, placed in a bowl on a table or a bookcase, tucked into storage cabinets. Wherever they are, they give off a lovely aroma that everyone will enjoy.

Heirloom Eggs

This egg makes a *very* special party favor—it will look wonderful when displayed on a table, under a ceiling light fixture, or in a window. This project does require a bit more time and patience than some of the other projects in this book. However, it is worth it, since it will last for years and provide as much pleasure to the recipient as it did to you while you were making it—I hope!

MATERIALS: Egg; model paints; fake pearl or ornamental bead; needle; nylon thread; newspapers.

INSTRUCTIONS: Poke holes with a needle at both ends of a raw egg. Blow out the inside of the egg into the sink. (This may take a little doing; be patient as you huff and puff into one hole and the egg yolk and white drip slowly out of the other hole.) When the egg is empty, gently wash and dry the shell. Spread newspapers on a working surface. When the egg is dry, paint a design on it. My favorite egg, painted by my daughter when she was ten or eleven years old, has pictures of the four seasons

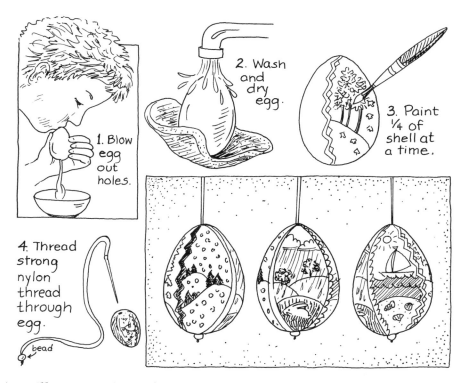

1. Blow egg out holes.

2. Wash and dry egg.

3. Paint ¼ of shell at a time.

4. Thread strong nylon thread through egg.

bead

(see illustration), and you can copy that. Or perhaps you will want to paint a green field on the bottom part of the egg, a blue sky on top, with flowers, sun, clouds, whatever, included in your own design. Paint one quarter of the shell at a time and let the painted area dry before you continue; don't try to paint the entire egg at once.

When all the paint has dried, thread a very fine needle with strong nylon thread. Double the thread and tie a good sturdy knot at the end. Put a bead, loose pearl, sequin, etc., on the thread near the knot. Insert the needle into the bottom hole of the egg. Jiggle it patiently upside down until the needle comes out at the other end. Pull it out, cut the thread off the needle, and tie it with a double or triple knot, leaving a loop long enough so that the egg can be hung from wherever one chooses.

About Gifts of Time

Here are suggestions for a different gift, an intangible but often even more appreciated present that requires nothing but your time, consideration, good sense, and love. You can plan these special gifts of time ahead of the day on which a holiday celebration or family gathering is to be held. They can also be spontaneous gestures of care and affection, unplanned, unbidden, and yet very welcome.

A gift of time to your mom or dad, sister or brother, before and during a holiday or special celebration can be the best present of all. That's when everyone is rushed, harassed, and even grouchy, and that's when everyone needs help the most. Your gift can be as simple as offering to clean out the car, sort out the mess in a kitchen cabinet, take your sister's books back to the library, or oil your brother's squeaky bike. Just put a card or a note making your offer under a parent's, brother's, or sister's pillow, on his or her plate, on the bathroom mirror, in a briefcase, school bag, or lunch box.

Spend time with a member of your family during holidays, or on his or her birthday, doing something he or she likes even if you don't. If your sister likes basketball and you love ballet, watch a game with her and learn the fine points of the game. Or play a board game that your kid brother loves and you usually refuse to touch. Sharing an activity with someone who cares about it will show that you care about the person.

Make a general offer of a gift of time to a relative, friend, or neighbor even if you don't know just what may be welcomed. Write a card, with a border of question marks, that says something like: I'D LOVE TO DO SOMETHING SPECIAL FOR YOU! MAY I MOW YOUR LAWN? WALK YOUR DOG? GO MARKETING? Give the card as a party favor or mail it as a greeting before a holiday, birthday, anniversary, etc.

Make a specific offer of a gift of time if you think you know what may be needed or wanted by the recipient. If your aunt and uncle are planning a vacation, and they have a houseful of plants, offer to water them while they are away. If your neighbors are going to visit distant family over the holidays, and they have gerbils or fish, a bird or a cat, offer to stop in each day to feed their pets. Make your offer on a card decorated with appropriate pictures cut out of magazines. Put the card in an envelope, address it to the lucky recipient, and place it on his or her plate, tuck it in his or her napkin at the party table, present it as you say good-by at the end of the party, or send it by mail.

When your gift is accepted, make arrangements that will be not only helpful to the recipient but comfortable and hassle-free for you. Find out whether the cat should be fed always at the same time, if the plants need to be watered every day, whether the lights in the house are preset to go on automatically each night, etc. And learn as much as you can beforehand about how the person likes things to be handled. Asking questions not only shows you care, but can avoid trouble later.

Spend time with a new kid on your block or in school. The time before and during holidays can be very lonely for someone who is new to your community. Why not offer to do something special together? You could plan a trip to the zoo, or offer to help him or her with the social studies diorama or the science program research. If he or she is of a different nationality, color, or religion, perhaps the two of you can share your customs and observances. Visit a synagogue if you've never been in one and ask your friend to come with you to services at your church. Let your new neighbor or schoolmate introduce you to foods he or she loves and you have never tasted. It will be a gift to yourself as well as to the other person.

Offer to do volunteer work in your community center, church, synagogue, senior citizen center, or nursing home. This can be a wonderful gift of time to your community and to people you may or may not know. Simple things such as helping to stuff envelopes or pack food baskets for delivery to the homebound can bring great happiness to others and much satisfaction to you. (Perhaps you can discuss such an activity with one of your teachers or within a community service club in your school.) Talking to and visiting elderly and often lonely people before and during holidays will make the celebrations more special for you, and very, very special for them.

Remember a good old expression as you give gifts of yourself:

What you put behind you, you will find before you. . . .